CODER ACADEMY

CODER

IN TRAINING

CODER ACADEMY

STUDENT PASS

Name ....

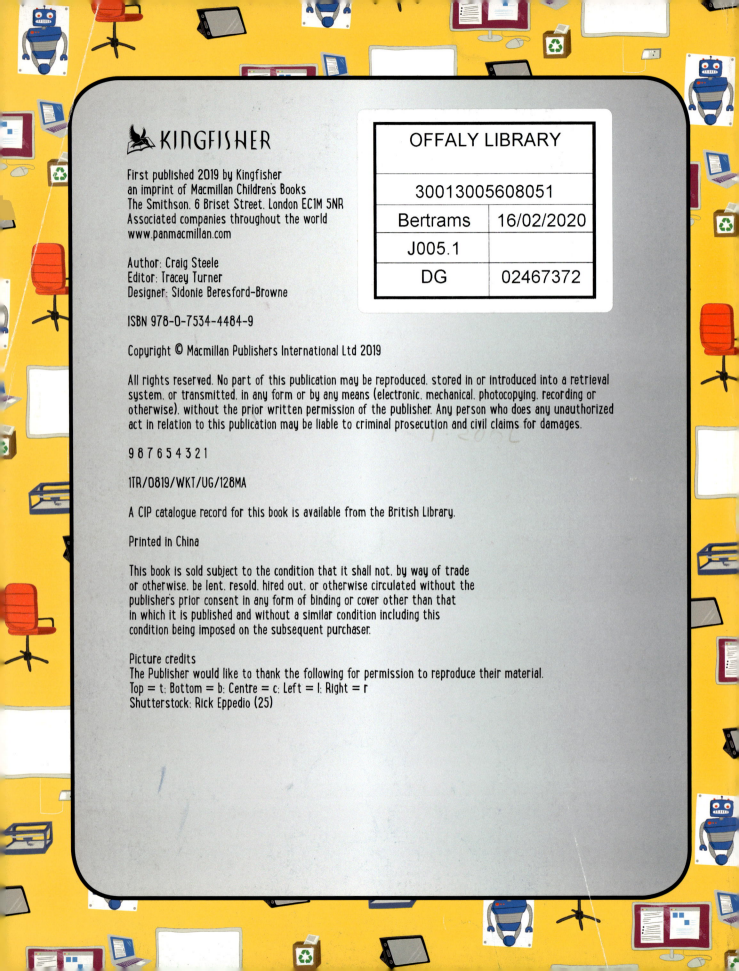

KINGFISHER

First published 2019 by Kingfisher
an imprint of Macmillan Children's Books
The Smithson. 6 Briset Street. London EC1M 5NR
Associated companies throughout the world
www.panmacmillan.com

Author: Craig Steele
Editor: Tracey Turner
Designer: Sidonie Beresford-Browne

ISBN 978-0-7534-4484-9

9 8 7 6 5 4 3 2 1

1TR/0819/WKT/UG/128MA

A CIP catalogue record for this book is available from the British Library.

Printed in China

Picture credits
The Publisher would like to thank the following for permission to reproduce their material.
Top = t: Bottom = b: Centre = c: Left = l: Right = r
Shutterstock: Rick Eppedio (25)

CODER

IN TRAINING

Can you find me
on every page?

KINGFISHER

CODING ACADEMY

TRAINING PROGRAMME

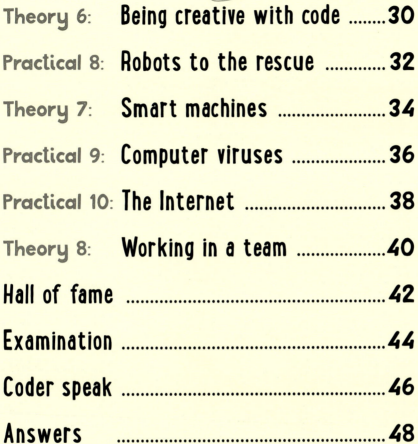

THEORY

THEORY pages are full of important information that you need to know.

PRACTICAL

PRACTICAL pages have a task to do or a coding skill to acquire. Tick each page when you have completed that part of your training.

TRAINING TIME

So, you want to be a coder? Do you love creating things using computers, tablets, and smartphones? Are you good at following instructions? Can you spot tiny mistakes that other people miss? You might just have what it takes.

WHAT MAKES A GOOD CODER?

It's not just about being able to use a computer, you need these other skills too:

A GOOD CODER ...

- ○ Is good at understanding instructions.
- ○ Is patient and doesn't just give up.
- ○ Thinks of new ways of doing things.
- ○ Enjoys solving problems using technology.
- ○ Tests what they make to make sure it works.

WHAT CAN YOU DO AS A COMPUTER CODER?

Lots of jobs need people who understand how to write code. You could use your digital skills to work on all sorts of exciting things.

DESIGN action-packed adventure games and apps.

FORECAST the weather.

BUILD tools for training athletes, helping them get faster or stronger.

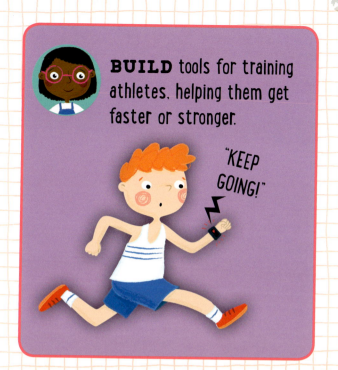

"KEEP GOING!"

WRITE code that keeps drivers safe.

MAKE security systems to protect the money in banks.

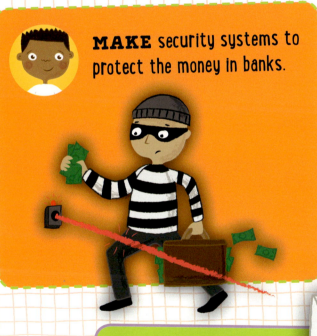

CREATE special effects with computer graphics.

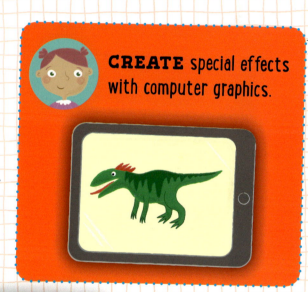

DEVISE equipment that helps perform scientific experiments.

PRACTICAL 1

CODING KIT

A coder can use lots of different gadgets to help them build games, apps, and websites. Before you start your coder training, you'll need to gather your tools.

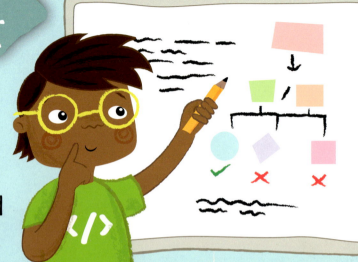

TECHIE TOOLS CHECKLIST

Find your coding kit in the office. Tick the box when you spot each one.

 ○ **Laptop** for when you need to work away from the desk

 ○ **Monitor** to show your work on a big screen

 ○ **3D printer** for creating small models

 ○ **Headphones** to let you work with sound files without annoying other people

 ○ **Whiteboard** for planning your ideas

 ○ **Laptop charger** to keep your battery topped up

 ○ **USB cables** to connect gadgets to your computer

 ○ **WiFi router** lets you connect to the Internet without wires.

Switch off computers when you're finished – it saves energy.

CODER'S TIPS

○ Look after expensive equipment and gadgets.

○ Keep an eye on your battery life, in case it runs out.

○ Remember to back up your files regularly.

○ Only use gadgets with an adult's permission.

○ Take regular breaks away from the computer.

Don't use broken or damaged equipment – recycle it instead.

THEORY 2

INSIDE A COMPUTER

It's useful for a coder to know a bit about what goes on inside a computer. Every part has to work together so that you can play a game or surf the web.

BLUETOOTH
This is used when connecting to wireless speakers, headphones, smart TVs, drones, or anything else with Bluetooth inside it.

TOUCH SCREEN
This shows the output from the computer. By touching this screen you can control the computer – this is called input.

CAMERA HOLE
Smile! Snap pictures using the camera. This is an example of input.

WIFI
Lets you connect to wireless networks.

PROCESSOR
This is the brain of the machine, which sends and receives messages from all other parts to make the computer complete tasks.

SPEAKERS
This is where the sound comes out. Sound is a type of output.

CIRCUITS
These lines connect different parts of the computer together. Information is sent along these wires.

HARD DRIVE
Where your files, photos, games, and apps are stored.

BATTERY
The bigger the battery, the longer it lasts between charges.

Are these items input devices, output devices, or both?

An output device sends information out from the computer.

QUIZ

Input devices are used to send information or instructions into a computer.

DEVICE	INPUT	OUTPUT
keyboard	○	○
speakers	○	○
mouse	○	○
touch screen	○	○
microphone	○	○

256GB

GIVING INSTRUCTIONS

Computer code is a list of instructions that tell a computer what to do. The instructions must be written in a computer programming language so the computer can understand it.

POPULAR COMPUTER PROGRAMMING LANGUAGES

- Python
- Scratch
- JavaScript
- Ruby
- C++

You'll see examples of computer code in this book. Although you will recognize some of the words, you won't understand the code unless you've learned the language.

The list of instructions that the computer can understand is called a **computer program**. Each instruction is called a **line of code**.

○ GET IT IN THE RIGHT ORDER

It's important to get the instructions in the right order. If you were coding a robot to bake a cake you'd make sure your code gives the instruction to crack the eggs before adding them to the bowl.

○ BE DETAILED

You need to give clear instructions so there is no chance of the computer misunderstanding you. For example, rather than just saying "add butter" your code would tell the robot exactly how much butter needs to be put in – "add 125g of unsalted butter".

ACTIVITY

Follow the instructions carefully to draw a shape. The instructions in the first box are written in English (for humans to read). The instructions in the second box are a computer program written in the Python programming language. Both of them do the same thing. What shape does it draw?

⭕ HUMAN INSTRUCTIONS

Pick up your pencil

Draw a horizontal line 5cm to the right

Keep your pencil on the paper

Draw a vertical line 5cm upwards

Keep your pencil on the paper

Draw a horizontal line 5cm to the left

Keep your pencil on the paper

Draw a vertical line 5cm downwards

⭕ COMPUTER CODE

```
import turtle
turtle.forward(5)
turtle.left(90)
turtle.forward(5)
turtle.left(90)
turtle.forward(5)
turtle.left(90)
turtle.forward(5)
```

PRACTICAL 3

DECISION-MAKING

Which route should you walk to school? Ham or cheese in your sandwich? Everyone has to make choices, and that's true for computer programs too. It's time to learn about how you code a computer to make decisions.

Coders can write code that tells the computer to follow different instructions depending on whether something is true or false. This is called a conditional statement.

Here's what a conditional statement looks like. It gives the computer a rule to follow.

If (something is true) then (do this), else (do that)

This will usually be a statement or a question with a true or false answer.

If the statement is true, follow these instructions.

Otherwise, follow these instructions. Or do nothing.

So, for example:

If today is a weekday, then get dressed for school, else get dressed for the park.

SATURDAY

When you're writing computer code, it works in the same way. See if you can work out what is happening in this code for a computer game.

```
if player.touches(coin) then {
    score = score + 20 }
if player.touches(fire) then {
    lives = lives - 1 }
```

If the player grabs a gold coin, their score will increase by 20 points.

If the player accidentally touches the fire they'll lose a life.

Computer code is often written with each instruction on a separate line. This helps make it easier for humans to read and follow the code.

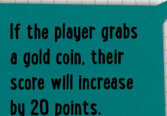

ACTIVITY

Here is the menu for the Coder Cafe.

Can you complete the blanks in these conditional statements to help give instructions to the chef?

If today is Monday then the soup is _____

If the soup is _____ then the sandwich is ham

If yesterday's soup was chicken then today's sandwich is _____

CODER CAFE

	SOUP	SANDWICH
Monday:	Tomato	Cheese
Tuesday:	Lentil	Tuna
Wednesday:	Pea	Cheese
Thursday:	Chicken	Ham
Friday:	Minestrone	Cheese

LOOPS

Instead of telling a computer to do the same thing several times, coders use a cool trick called a loop. The loop tells the computer to repeat certain lines of code, rather than giving the instruction over and over again.

So for example, say you were washing three mugs:

INSTRUCTIONS WITHOUT A LOOP:
- Wash a mug
  Dry the mug
  Put the mug away
  Wash a mug
  Dry the mug
  Put the mug away
  Wash a mug
  Dry the mug
  Put the mug away

INSTRUCTIONS USING A LOOP:

Do this 3 times:
 Wash a mug
 Dry the mug
 Put the mug away

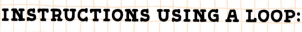

The second code using a loop is shorter and easier to read. It still does the same thing.

WHILE LOOPS

Sometimes you don't know exactly how many times you want the loop to repeat the code. In those situations you use a "while loop". This keeps repeating the instructions until the task is complete.

For example, here is a "while loop" for scanning groceries at the supermarket checkout.

The loop keeps repeating until there are no items in the basket.

While there are still items in the basket:

Pick up an item
Scan the item
Put the item in the shopping bag

These are the instructions that are repeated.

ACTIVITY

Now it's your turn to write a loop. Can you complete these instructions so that the computer knows to set the dinner table for 4 guests?

Do this _____ times:
Place the plate in the middle
Place the fork on the _____
Place the _____ on the right

Coders call mistakes in their code "bugs". These bugs mean their apps, games or websites don't work the way they are meant to. A clever coder can track down these mistakes and fix them. It's time to go on a bug hunt!

DEBUGGING

SYNTAX BUGS

These are the most common types of bugs. They are usually caused by a typing mistake. Luckily they are easy to fix if you can spot them.

Go to the bus stop

Can you spot the syntax bug in these instructions?

While the school bus hasn't arrived:
Wait for the school bus

Get on the skool bus

While the bus hasn't arrived at the school:
Sit in your seat

Get off the school bus

LOGIC BUGS

These types of bugs happen when the instructions are in the wrong order. To find these bugs coders must look very carefully at their code step by step.

Can you spot the logic bug in these instructions?

Get out of bed

Put your underwear on

Put your trousers on

Put your jumper on

Put your shoes on

Put your socks on

Eat breakfast

19

TESTING CODE

Before launching an app, a good coder runs tests to make sure everything works as it is supposed to. This is the best way to find the bugs in the code. Here's how to become an expert tester.

TEST PLAN

Code testers make a "test plan". This outlines what they are going to test, and what they expect to happen when they run the test. That way they can tell if the app has passed or failed.

Your new app is for booking cinema tickets. These tests could be part of your test plan:

NORMAL VALUES

You put in something reasonable that the app should be able to handle. You might use the app to try to book two cinema tickets and see if it works:

Number of tickets [2]

BOOK NOW

✏️ ACTIVITY

You've been asked to test an app that counts how many sweets someone eats during a film. At the end of the film, the app user must enter the number of sweets they have eaten from a packet of 10 sweets, so the number is expected to be between 0 and 10.

Match these input values with the type of test:

INPUT VALUES

3 sweets

!!@@

16 sweets

TEST TYPE

Abnormal values

Extreme values

Normal values

EXTREME VALUES

This is when you test the biggest and smallest amounts the app should be able to deal with. Your cinema app is meant to let you book between 1 and 8 tickets, so you should try to book:

1 ticket	0 tickets
8 tickets	9 tickets

These should be accepted.

These should be rejected.

Number of tickets **9**

BOOK NOW

ABNORMAL VALUES

This is when you do something totally unexpected. For example, rather than typing in the number of tickets you want you might type the name of the film. The app should reject this because it's a letter not a number.

Number of tickets **a**

BOOK NOW

SPOTTING PATTERNS

A key skill for a clever coder is being able to spot patterns. When you're faced with a coding problem it's helpful to ask yourself "Where have I seen something similar before?". You might realize the new problem is actually very similar to another problem you've already solved.

WHAT'S NEXT?

These sequences follow a pattern, each number goes up by 2. By spotting this pattern it means you can work out what comes next.

The next number would be 12.

0 2 4 6 8 10

This pattern is a little more complicated.

But this handy table makes it easy to understand. Using the table you can see the next shape would be a red flower.

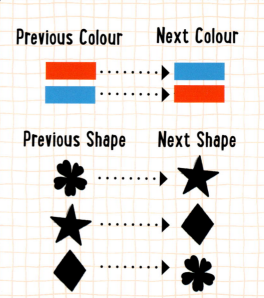

Previous Colour	Next Colour
red	blue
blue	red

Previous Shape	Next Shape
flower	star
star	diamond
diamond	flower

Use your pattern recognition skills to pair up the matching butterflies.

PRACTICAL NO: 6

tick here

APPROVED

BINARY CODE

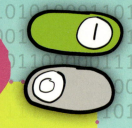

Now that you know a bit about computer programming, it's time to learn about the way a machine stores information.

Computers are made up of lots of electronic switches that can either be on or off. In binary, on is represented by a 1 and off is represented by a 0. So to tell a computer which switches are on and which are off, a binary digit is either a 1 or a 0.

Binary is a different system of counting from the one we're used to.

We're used to decimals so binary looks weird.

This is the decimal system we use:

1000s	100s	10s	1s
0	1	1	0

These numbers show what each column represents.

We have no thousands, one hundred, one ten and no ones. So the number on the left is a hundred plus ten – a hundred and ten (110). We could put a 3 in the 100s, a 4 in the 10s, and a 5 in the 1s columns – that would be three hundred and forty-five (345).

THEORY NO: 4
tick here
APPROVED

But the binary system works like this:

8s	4s	2s	1s
0	1	1	0

We have no eights, one four, one two and no ones. So as a decimal number, this binary number is four plus two – six. We can't put in any other numbers but 1s and 0s, so we have to make a long line of digits to make big numbers. Each column doubles the value of the previous column: 1000 is 8, and 10000 is 16.

All of this is made from 1s and 0s!

BINARY FACT

A "bit" in computer programming is short for "binary digit" – a 1 or a 0.
The number 5 is 0101, that's 4 "bits" in size.

BINARY NUMBERS

Decimal		Binary
0	=	0000
1	=	0001
2	=	0010
3	=	0011
4	=	0100
5	=	0101
6	=	0110
7	=	0111
8	=	1000
9	=	1001
10	=	1010

This table shows the binary code used to represent the numbers 0 to 10. The decimal number is the one we'd normally use as humans. The binary number is the way that number is stored so the computer understands it.

ACTIVITY

Can you work out the binary number for the decimal number 12?

STORING IMAGES

Now you know how numbers can be stored using binary code, but what about pictures? On a computer screen, images are made up of tiny dots called "pixels". To store the image, each pixel is represented by a binary number.

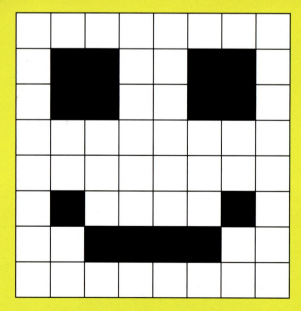

○ If you look at a picture on a computer screen closely you'll see rows and rows of pixels.

○ In a black and white image, each pixel is either 1 (black) or 0 (white).

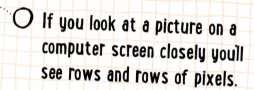

0	0	0	0	0	0	0	0
0	1	1	0	0	1	1	0
0	1	1	0	0	1	1	0
0	0	0	0	0	0	0	0
0	0	0	0	0	0	0	0
0	1	0	0	0	0	1	0
0	0	1	1	1	1	0	0
0	0	0	0	0	0	0	0

In a colour image, each pixel can have a different binary number that means a specific colour.

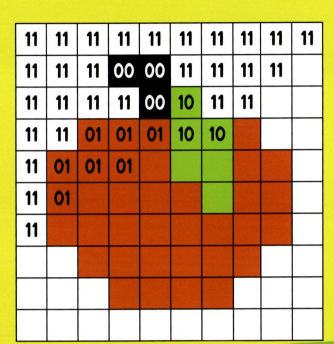

11	11	11	11	11	11	11	11	11	11
11	11	11	00	00	11	11	11	11	
11	11	11	11	00	10	11	11		
11	11	01	01	01	10	10			
11	01	01	01						
11	01								
11									

01 =

10 =

00 =

11 =

Smartphones and digital cameras often save photos as JPEG files. These are a type of bitmap image.

ACTIVITY

What images do these bitmaps represent? Make your own grid and draw a black box for each 1, and leave the 0 boxes blank.

a)

1	1	0	0	0
0	1	0	0	0
0	1	0	0	0
0	1	1	1	0
0	1	0	1	0

b)

0	1	0	1	0
1	1	1	1	1
1	1	1	1	1
0	1	1	1	0
0	0	1	0	0

TURTLE GRAPHICS

Turtle graphics is a popular way of creating graphics with computer code. Coders write programs that give instructions to a virtual turtle that moves around the screen drawing shapes.

Coders give instructions like "move forward" or "turn 90 degrees to the left" to tell the turtle how to move. The code has to be written in a special way for the computer to understand it. As the turtle moves it draws a line.

Here's some simple code to make a turtle draw a line.

```
import turtle
tom = turtle.Turtle()
tom.forward(50)
```

Create a new turtle.

This one is named Tom.

Tom the turtle to move 50 pixels in the direction he is facing.

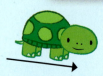

90° – or ninety degrees – is this angle. If you're facing the top of the page and turn 90° to the right, you'll be facing the right-hand edge of the page.

Here's another example of Tom the turtle drawing a triangle.

```
import turtle
tom = turtle.Turtle()
tom.forward(100)
tom.left(90)
tom.forward(100)
tom.left(135)
tom.forward(142)
```

Tom starts here.

Turtle graphics can be used to draw some amazing shapes. Look at these examples.

BEING CREATIVE WITH CODE

CREATE ART

P5.js is coding tool that lets you create spectacular visual art using computer code. Just by using a few lines of code you can draw shapes, generate patterns, and fill the screen with exciting animations.

You can use your coding skills to be creative. Digital artists and composers use computer code to create amazing new pieces of art and music.

This pattern is created using these 10 lines of code.

The coded instructions tell the computer to draw rectangles repeatedly in a circle to create a pattern. Every rectangle's colour is chosen randomly, either red, yellow or orange. So every time you run the program you get a different pattern – your own unique artwork.

```
var a = 0;
var choose = 0;
var list = ['red','yellow','orange']
function setup(){createCanvas(900,900);}
function draw(){
    choose = int(random(list.length));
    fill(list[choose]);
    translate(450,450);
    rotate(a++);
    rect(a%333,0,a%33,5+a%10);}
```

MAKE MUSIC

Sonic Pi lets you create sound and music. The code tells the computer the type of sound to make: how loud it should be, how long it should last, how high or low it should be. You can code everything from simple tunes to more complicated tracks with lots of layers of sound.

THEORY NO: 6

tick here

APPROVED

This Sonic Pi code uses a loop. Every time it goes through the loop it will play either a drum sound effect or a snare.

You don't need to be able to play an instrument to code your own masterpiece.

```
loop do
    if tick.even?
        sample :bd_haus
    else
        sample :sn_dub
    end
    sleep 0.5
end
```

ROBOTS TO THE RESCUE

Robots can be programmed to help in situations that are too dangerous for humans. Maybe you'll use your coding skills to program a life-saving robot?

Flying drone robots put out fires in places too hot for humans to go.

Robots help medics get into and out of protective clothing. This helps make sure they can change equipment safely and without spreading germs.

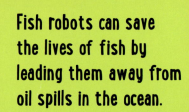

Fish robots can save the lives of fish by leading them away from oil spills in the ocean.

ACTIVITY

START

Put these instructions in the right order to program the fire-fighting robot to move through the building putting out the fires.

- Move forward 1 step
- Move forward 2 steps
- Turn Right
- Move forward 1 step
- Turn Left
- Turn Right
- Move forward 1 step
- Turn Right
- Turn Left
- Move forward 2 steps
- Move forward 3 steps
- Turn Right

SMART MACHINES

Artificial Intelligence (or AI for short) is an exciting area of technology. Coders who work on these projects create programs that try to think like a human. These are often called smart technologies.

How can AI help?

FINDING PEOPLE JOBS

AI programs try to match someone's skills and interests with the job most suited to them. They can even make sure the job isn't too far away from where the person lives.

PARKING A CAR

Smart cars use cameras and bump sensors to easily park themselves in tight spaces that humans would struggle with.

MEAL IDEAS

Tell an AI program what food you've got in the fridge, and then it recommends a healthy recipe using those ingredients. Perfect for when you can't decide what you want for dinner.

TO: ALFIE

Hi Alfie
Do you want to go to the park tomorrow?

WRITING YOUR EMAILS

AI programs can make it faster to write email messages by suggesting words or phrases to include. These programs learn by reading over your past messages, so they can work out what you might say next.

ACTIVITY

Artificially Intelligent programs can be used to make recommendations. They might suggest a movie to watch, or new music to listen to. One way they can do this is by asking questions.

Follow the flowchart below and find out which book the AI recommends you read next.

Do you want to read something exciting or something scary?

EXCITING

Should the main character be magical, or true to life?

SCARY

Should the story take place in the past or the future?

PAST

This spooky Victorian ghost story will give you the chills.

FUTURE

A scary story in space, with an alien hunting down the crew of a spaceship, is the perfect story for you.

MAGIC

You should read this fantasy story, filled with wizards, knights, and castles.

TRUE

You'd love this action and adventure story about an archaeogolist hunting for treasures around the world.

COMPUTER VIRUSES

It's time to find out about computer viruses – nasty computer programs that are made by cyber criminals who want to damage other people's computers or steal the information on them.

WORM

This virus keeps making copies of itself. It then sends itself to other computers to infect them too. All the extra copies waste storage space and make the computer very slow.

TROJAN HORSE

A virus disguised as another app. It's named after an Ancient Greek story where soldiers sneaked into the city of Troy by hiding inside a giant wooden horse. When a user is tricked into opening the disguised program, the virus activates.

RANSOMWARE

Cyber criminals can use a virus to scramble a computer's files. They'll only give the user the key to unscramble the files if they pay them money.

HOW DOES ANTIVIRUS WORK?

An antivirus app has a big list of viruses and worms that it knows about. If it finds any of them in the computer it gets rid of them. It's important to use the latest version of the app so the list is up to date.

! PROTECTING YOURSELF

O Turn on antivirus software.

O Don't open apps or files that look suspicious.

O Only visit websites or use apps that a grown-up has let you use.

MOST WANTED LIST

These are some of the offending viruses that your antivirus software should track down and remove.

ILOVEYOU

Shamoon

WannaCry

(Ransomware example)

Stuxnet

(Trojan horse example)

Blaster

(Worm example)

1

2

REMEMBER

It's against the law to make a computer virus or send them to other people on purpose.

FIND THE VIRUS

Can you spot the Trojan horse? One of these apps has been replaced with a virus that's pretending to be the real thing.

3

4

THE INTERNET

1

The Internet is a network made up of millions of computers that are connected to each other, and can share or send messages, photos, music, and other files. Coders build the apps that allow us to connect and share over the Internet.

2

3

WHAT CAN YOU DO ON THE INTERNET?

○ GO SHOPPING
You can buy almost anything on the Internet – books, toys, clothes, even pizza!

○ PLAY GAMES
Compete against other gamers from around the world. Online games can sometimes have hundreds of people playing at the same time.

c

4

a

b

d

ACTIVITY

There are real, physical cables connecting all the major parts of the Internet. Can you match up the connected pairs on this map?

○ SEE A DOCTOR

A doctor can see a patient and give them advice over a video call – good news for people who live far away from a doctor's surgery.

○ KEEP IN TOUCH

Emails, video chats, and voice calls are just some of the ways you can catch up with friends and family online.

○ TRAVEL THE WORLD

Online maps mean you can go sightseeing without ever leaving your home.

WORKING IN A TEAM

Coders work with other people to make amazing digital products. You'll have to work with other talented team members with their own special skills – or maybe one of these jobs is for you?

DESIGNER

Designers are in charge of the way an app looks. If you love drawing your ideas you might like this job.

PROJECT MANAGER

This person makes sure apps are made on time. They work out who needs to do what, and then make sure it happens. They're usually very organized and good at encouraging other people in the team.

TESTER

This person looks for all the bugs in an app. Testers try using the app in lots of different ways to see if they can break it.

MARKETING MANAGER

Marketing people are brilliant at making adverts and selling – once you've made an app, you need someone who can tell people how good it is and encourage them to buy it.

FINANCE OFFICER

Finance staff look after everything to do with money. They make sure teams have enough cash, and that the apps bring in money for the business.

Which job do you think might be best for you?

CUSTOMER SUPPORT

If a customer has a problem with an app they'll need someone who can help. Customer support staff need to be patient and enjoy fixing things.

COMPANIES BIG AND SMALL

You could make and release an app all by yourself – but then you'd need to be good at doing all the jobs! Large companies making apps have thousands of workers doing different jobs.

THEORY NO: 8

tick here

APPROVED

41

ADA LOVELACE

A mathematician and the first computer programmer. In the 1800s, before the first computer was built, she wrote a program that showed how a machine could be used to do difficult maths.

GRACE HOPPER

A rear Admiral in the US navy and a computer programmer. She created a tool that translated computer programming languages into code a machine can understand.

MARGARET HAMILTON

A computer scientist. She was head of the team that wrote the code for the first ever Moon landing in 1969.

DONA BAILEY

A gamer and computer programmer. She was the first woman to create an arcade video game.

HALL OF FAME

TIM BERNERS-LEE

A computer scientist. He invented the World Wide Web - now we use it to share information around the world.

LARRY PAGE AND SERGEY BRIN

Larry and Sergey started the company Google. The Google search engine is the most popular way to find things on the web.

GUIDO VAN ROSSUM

The author of the Python programming language. Python can be used to build games, make apps, and even control robots.

HIDEO KOJIMA

A video game designer and director who is best known for making action and adventure games.

These computer scientists have changed the world using technology. After your training, maybe you'll join them?

EXAMINATION

Take this exam to see how much you have learned.

1 What is the role of the computer processor?
- a) It is the brain of the machine
- b) It stores the data
- c) The sound comes out of it

2 Which of these is an example of an input device?
- a) LED screen
- b) Keyboard
- c) Speaker

3 What do coders call mistakes in their code?
- a) Gnats
- b) Insects
- c) Bugs

4 What is the binary code for 4?
- a) 0010
- b) 0100
- c) 1100

5 Which of these is NOT a computer program used by cyber criminals?
- a) Virus
- b) Trojan horse
- c) Goblin

6 In computing, what do the letters AI stand for?
- a) Advanced Information
- b) Artificial Intelligence
- c) Automatic Ice cream

7 Which of these is a coding tool for creating music?
- a) Sound Mash
- b) Sonic Pi
- c) Cobra Chords

8 What does a good coder do with their code before releasing it?
- a) Tickle it
- b) Tackle it
- c) Test it

9 What is the pattern of this sequence: 5, 10, 15, 20 ?

a) The numbers go up by 5

b) The numbers go down by 5

c) The numbers stay the same

10 Which of these can you use to connect a gadget to a computer?

a) Copper rope

b) USB cable

c) Magnetic tape

11 Which statement is TRUE?

a) Images on a computer screen are made up of dots called pixels

b) Sounds on a computer are made up of noises called pixels

12 What activity does this loop describe?

While there are books on the floor:

Pick up a book

Put it on the shelf

a) Picking up two books from the floor

b) Moving all the books from the floor onto the shelf

13 A list of instructions the computer can understand is called a _____. Each instruction is called a line of _____.

a) Document/sentence

b) Song/notes

c) Computer program/code

CODING SCORES

Check your answers at the back of the book and add up your score.

1 to 5 Oops! Go back and swot up on your coding facts.

6 to 10 You are well on your way to becoming a top coder.

11 to 13 Top of the class! You really know your stuff!

CODER SPEAK

android
A robot designed to look and behave like a human.

app
A computer program you can install on a smartphone or tablet, short for "application".

artificial intelligence
A computer program that tries to copy the way a human thinks.

binary digit
Either a 1 or a 0, sometimes shortened to "bit".

bugs
Mistakes in computer code that cause problems.

compiler
A tool that translates code into machine language t he computer understands.

computer code
A set of detailed instructions that tell a computer what to do.

drone
A flying robot controlled remotely by a human or smart enough to fly on its own.

integer
A whole number: 1, 15, 26, -45, and 100 are all integers.

loop
Used by coders to repeat a section of code.

operating system
The main program on a computer that helps all the hardware and software work together.

processor
The brain of a computer. Powerful computers have a fast processor inside them.

Python
A popular and free programming language that uses English words and text.

Scratch
A programming language that uses blocks of code and doesn't require much typing. Good for beginners.

CODER ACADEMY

WELL DONE!

You made it through your coder training.

Name...

FULLY QUALIFIED

CODER

ANSWERS

Page 8

The things to find are circled below.

Page 10

Keyboard: input: speakers: output: mouse: input: touch screen: input and output: microphone: input.

Page 13

The shape is a square.

Page 15

The missing words are:
  tomato
  chicken
  cheese

Page 17

Do this ④ times:
  Place the (fork) on the (left)
  Place the (knife) on the right

Page 18

Look at the third instruction down: "school" is spelt wrongly as "skool".

Page 19

The instructions tell you to put your shoes on before your socks.

Page 21

3 sweets – Normal values
!!@@ – Abnormal values
16 sweets – Extreme values

Page 23

Page 25

1100 is 12 in binary.

Page 27

a)
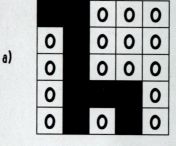

b)
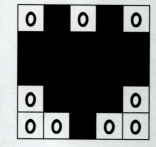

Pages 33

Turn Left
Move forward 2 steps
Turn Right
Move forward 1 step
Turn Left
Move forward 1 step
Turn Right
Move forward 2 steps
Turn Right
Move forward 3 steps
Turn Right
Move forward 1 step

Pages 37

Number 4 is the Trojan horse – the rocket ship window is different from the others.

Pages 38–39

1 = c: 2 = b: 3 = a: 4 = d.

Pages 44–45

1 = a: 2 = b: 3 = c: 4 = b: 5 = c:
6 = b: 7 = b: 8 = c: 9 = a: 10 = b:
11 = a: 12 = b: 13 = c.